THE NEXT BEND IN THE ROAD

PHOENIX **POETS**

MICHAEL FRIED

The Next Bend in the Road

THE UNIVERSITY OF CHICAGO PRESS

Chicago and London

MICHAEL FRIED is the J. R. Herbert Boone Professor of
Humanities at the Johns Hopkins University, where he also
directs the Humanities Center.

The University of Chicago Press, Chicago 60637
The University of Chicago Press, Ltd., London
© 2004 by The University of Chicago
All rights reserved. Published 2004
Printed in the United States of America

13 12 11 10 09 08 07 06 05 04   1 2 3 4 5

ISBN: 0-226-26323-1 (cloth)
ISBN: 0-226-26325-8 (paper)

Library of Congress Cataloging-in-Publication Data
Fried, Michael
    The next bend in the road / Michael Fried.
       p.   cm.—(Phoenix poets)
    ISBN: 0-226-26323-1 (cloth: alk. paper)
    ISBN: 0-226-26325-8 (paper: alk. paper)
    I. Title. II. Series.
  PS3556.R48825N49 2004
  811'.54—dc22
                                                    2003017621

to Ruth and Anna

All that we can say is that everything is arranged in this life as though we entered it carrying a burden of obligations contracted in a former life; there is no reason inherent in the conditions of life on this earth that can make us consider ourselves obliged to do good, to be kind and thoughtful, even to be polite, nor for an atheist artist to consider himself obliged to begin over again a score of times a piece of work the admiration aroused by which will matter little to his worm-eaten body, like the patch of yellow wall painted with so much skill and refinement by an artist destined to be for ever unknown and barely identified under the name Vermeer. All these obligations, which have no sanction in our present life, seem to belong to a different world, a world based on kindness, scrupulousness, self-sacrifice, a world entirely different from this one and which we leave in order to be born on this earth, before perhaps returning there to live once again beneath the sway of those unknown laws which we obeyed because we bore their precepts in our hearts, not knowing whose hand had traced them there—those laws to which every profound work of the intellect brings us nearer and which are invisible only—if then!—to fools.

— MARCEL PROUST, *The Captive*

Contents

II THE NEXT BEND IN THE ROAD

III A SUMMER NIGHT

Acknowledgments

Grateful acknowledgment is made to the editors of the journals in which these poems, or versions of them, first appeared:

American Poetry Review: "The Chase"; "Due North"; " 'The Earthquake in Chile' "; "Full Moonlight"; "Gisèle Lestrange"; "The Hilltop"; "Kafka's Drawings"; "A Night at the Opera"; "The Yellow Dress" (as " 'Phèdre' ") ; "Tsvetayeva's Letters"
London, Review of Books: "The Tunnel"
The New Republic: "The Next Bend in the Road"
The Paris Review: "The End of History"
Raritan: "Greek Restaurant"; "A Summer Night"
The Southern Review: "The Curvature of the Earth"; " 'Le Déjeuner sur l'herbe' "
Salmagundi: "Freud's Sacrifice"; *"Noa-Noa"*; "The Visitor from the Future"; "The Wound"

*

Heartfelt thanks to two friends, Allen Grossman and John Harbison, for their counsel and encouragement. And to an absent third, the late Ian Hamilton, for his brotherhood in the art. Finally, I'm grateful to James Welling—also a friend, I'm happy to say—for allowing me to use one of his superb degradés on the cover of this book.

I THE SEND-OFF

The Send-Off

The hummingbird looks up from his flower punchbowl with an expression of
    pure dazzlement.
The May morning is that perfect,
our eleven-month-old daughter in her Grandma's-gift raspberry sundress is
    that astonishing.

She came here in stages
from Wuhan, China, where we adopted her
in the eye of a cyclone.

En route from the orphanage
all the while Anna slept in your arms
her birth mother's tears rose wavelike from the dusty earth
to speed us on our way.

Days of the Comet

I

Your mouth opens
in a disbelieving laugh
as tears stream down your face.
Definitely excess of joy.

II

The snipers are gone
from their leafy beds above the city.
(So too are the elms
that lined the boulevards.)

III

In the Northern sky
a never before seen comet
approaches earth
near the century's end.

IV

Let the heavy oar doze in its oarlock.
It is time
to seek the poem
with both hands!

The Alhambra

The summer I was twenty-two I hitchhiked from Fuengirola to Granada, and spent several ardent, unforgettable days at the Alhambra. Mainly just walking up and down and seeing, or finding a secluded spot in which to read the great modern Spanish poets I had recently come to love—Jiménez, Machado, Lorca. The sun exploding continuously in a cobalt sky made the simplest nouns incandesce: *hombre, caballo, sueño, naranja, muerte.* Hour after hour I inhaled the exotic blossoms of the Generalife, descended with icy waters from the Sierra Nevada, contemplated in a kind of rapture the carved stucco tracery that (I later learned) everywhere intricately repeated the name of God until there was no space for anything else. Sail-shaped and starlike colored tiles fitted together unexpectedly, like noon and midnight, conquest and silence. I knew I couldn't stay forever, in fact I had to leave almost at once, but part of me, a scrap of my immortal soul, was unwilling to accept this and remained behind: a small mongrel dog, quick enough not to get caught, wandering aimlessly in shadows that are filled with light.

The Tunnel

To be nothing but fire
not even the fuel that feeds it

wasn't my father's style.
When the time came for him to die

(of a cirrhotic liver
caused by poisoned blood

flushed through him one winter dawn
to fight a bleeding ulcer)

he found a stone wall
with, at its base, a tunnel

just too narrow to admit
a man. Undaunted he crawled through

hand over hand
to the other side.

April 4, 1968

I remember that day;
I remember crying hysterically.
It remains the worst day in my life
not directly personal.

When the day ended the sun went down,
stars came out, flames leaped heavenward.
He had been to the mountain top but we,
we had not.

April 4, 1998

In the White Swan Hotel, Guangzhou

A man who thinks he is my father
gazes at the traffic on the Pearl River.

A woman who first took me in her arms yesterday
looks down at me and cries with joy.

I don't know what choices I have
other than to bestow or withhold my love.

I'll wait until I can understand
their foreign, passionate speech and then we'll see.

The Kites

Our first walk with Anna in the park in Wuhan. Old men with tiny fishing rods fly exquisite bird-shaped kites (but there are no birds) in the dazzling void. They smile when they see us, we approach them, by a heroic feat of mutual comprehension it becomes clear that they approve of what we are there for once they are assured she is not a boy.

Greek Restaurant

You had steered us to a simple Greek restaurant
others must have taken you to
because once matters became serious
we never went back.

I remember feeling:
if only I could touch—stroke—your arms
just below the shoulders.
They were athletic,

slim, perfectly poised.
I dared imagine no more brazen act
than that, that I might stroke your arms.

And then what? I had no idea,
my imagination was left so far behind by my desire
as it stormed ahead, into the dark.

Cézanne

Returning home
from a day spent looking at paintings
I'm as exhausted
as I would be if I had dug a trench

Returning home
from a day spent digging trenches
the painter pulls the brim of his derby
low over his eyes

Passing each other
on a narrow road
I nod to him in my friendliest manner
he glares at me with what's left of his face

Care

for Allen Grossman

I

The badger knows several great artists
intimately. This is said without irony;
he thinks of them as great because they have made numinous paintings
    and sculptures
that will last thousands of years if care is taken of them.
But will care be taken of them?
The badger is worried.

II

He has an older friend who collects ancient pots.
The friend is a poet, of a breed altogether beyond the badger's comprehension,
who spends hours looking at the pots
admiring their form and markings, and imagining
how they were once used.
                  In the dimness of predawn
the poet's apartment is like a cave
in neolithic China, minus the harsh rich smell
of burning dung.

III

Recently the poet acquired another pot,
minuscule, exquisite. Of hard gray stone
worked to absolute smoothness.
Egyptian.

He is convinced it was a scribe's inkwell.
When the time comes he will dip his pen in it
to write his gravest
songs.

Kafka's Drawings

It turns out that Kafka always wanted to draw, "to hold fast to what was seen," as he put it. He also said of the little cartoon-like men in his drawings: "They come out of the dark to vanish into the dark." And: "My drawing is a perpetually renewed and unsuccessful attempt at primitive magic." Was he dismayed by that unsuccess? It seems not—he accepted without complaint that his drawings' magic was imperfect, that between the pencil in his hand and the sheet of paper on his desk something intervened to derail his best efforts to capture the shapes of life in their endlessly seductive but also undeniably comic, therefore inescapably tragic, vitality. The surviving drawings suggest, against all likelihood, that it was precisely the dimension—the perspective—of the tragic that eluded him.

The Realm of Spirit

When I wrote my poems and kept them in a drawer
I believed I was William Blake in a closet.

The pathos of my unappreciated genius
bowed my shoulders but put spring in my step.

In that divided mood each line I composed
seemed to me a triumph against prodigious odds.

I communicated this sense of struggle to my friends
who treated me with the respect due a warrior.

And I exhaled contempt for the famous names
whose anodyne verses collected yearly prizes.

I lived like that for decades, impregnable
in the knowledge that my castle had no drawbridge.

Then one day in a trance of inadvertence
I sent my poems to an editor, who published them.

Now the drawer is empty and the closet is sealed
and I know that in the realm of spirit I am nothing.

The Chase

In the Asian galleries of the Seattle Art Museum I discover a painting on silk and, almost, a prose poem. The painting, by Li Anzhong (active 1120–1160), is of a hawk chasing a pheasant. The almost-poem—the wall label—reads: "The desperate situation of the pheasant is emphasized by its gasping mouth, and the hawk's determination is conveyed through its raised neck and tightly closed beak. The brushwork is so subtle and light, however, that the chase is imbued with a dreamlike quality." What the label doesn't say (I glimpse it in the hawk's ruby eye) is that in the merest fraction of a second the unfair chase will be consummated dream or no dream.

Before a Duel

The snow was so deep the seconds in their heavy boots had to tramp it down for almost an hour before there was a clear field of fire. At a proper, i.e. simultaneously respectful and contemptuous, distance from each other the intended combatants sat waiting, one smoking a long thin clay pipe, the other paring and eating an apple. Both were wrapped in monumental *pelisses* that gave them the deceptive appearance of friendly bears but can hardly be imagined to have made them indifferent to the subarctic cold. Both followed to the letter the agreed upon script: throughout the lengthy preliminaries neither so much as glanced in the other's direction. Even then and there men felt it would be interesting to know what one of them was thinking.

Papyrus

Lubricated in fish blood, tears, semen.

The Drought

We wake in the dark
to great flashes of light.
The drought is history.

Each time the thunder
crashes the barn walls shake.
Is that our daughter crying?

No: she's sound asleep
in the arms of the storm.
Oh firm-fleshed Anna!

We stand over your crib
scarcely breathing.
Though we're not needed
our lives are complete.

The Rape of Nanking

Reading about the Rape of Nanking
my mind clouds over.

Tell me God how can human beings, even "hardened" soldiers, have done the
    things it's documented these did?
(And not in anger or sexual release but deliberately week after week.)

I ask this in all humility,
one killer to another.

The Glare

In Jerusalem
I stared through the noonday glare at the Western Wall.
I felt inside me no emotion
I could recognize.

Something stirred
in those lightstruck depths.
Breathed for only an instant and then died
baffled and helpless.

I shut my eyes
and counted to a thousand.
When I opened them nothing fundamental had changed
in the sky or on the ground.

The sun blazed.
On the stones powdering in the glare.
On the noonday religious rocking in their shoes.
On the unmoved visitor and unmoving dirt-colored personnel carrier taking
    everything in.

Gisèle Lestrange

For several years before she died we occasionally spent an evening in the company of Paul Celan's widow, the etcher Gisèle Lestrange. We met her first at a party thrown by Parisian friends to celebrate their engagement. She was charming, with the indefinable magnetism certain older cultivated European women possess whether or not they were beauties in their youth. And a great directness, which led her once when driving across the Seine in the company of an American translator to observe in an ordinary tone of voice that just below was where Celan had drowned himself. (Her words "took my breath away," the translator recalls.) Until that night I had never seen her etchings. Our friends owned three or four, and what surprised me was their restraint, as if the artist had been too familiar with the demands of art to wish to satisfy them completely. On closer view, the bite of the acid was everywhere deliberately reined in, not from excessive finesse but from an unwillingness to mark deeply. I thought: she has experienced illuminations she has no desire to impart other than by the faintest shiver of contrast.

Months later, after a chance meeting at a concert, Gisèle Lestrange came back to our recently acquired *pied-à-terre* and sat and talked for an hour over a glass of wine. Then I went down with her into rue Lafayette to help hail a taxi. Rain was falling, and it took a few minutes before I captured one and held the door open as she got in. That was the nearest I have come to touching poetry's hem.

The Meadow

Our joy is so great
it casts a shadow
across all the future
we dare to imagine

Nevertheless we cheer Anna on
as she toddles on sturdy legs
toward a sunlit meadow
in which we are not

Above the pines a red hawk
tracks her on a whim
I want to warn her, to call out,
but my voice is frozen

Carefree and high-stepping
Anna plunges ahead
Her mother too sees the hawk
Her tears flow in profusion

Our daughter hears them fall
Laughing she turns and waves
Hell raging in his heart
the red hawk sails out of sight

*　　*　　*

And now peaceful night
shakes out its many worlds
The meadow, the sunlit meadow,
will be back tomorrow

Due North

Oriented to the stars the poet marches briskly due north on a windy night in his fifty-eighth year. The sensory deprivation of Iowa City (in the words of his host) surrounds him on four sides, but who cares, it's pitch black and the wind is trampling on his face with such unbridled élan that he laughs out loud. A new, more refined intuition of mortality enters his heart like the blade of a spear on which has been engraved the figure of a heart.

The Dream

He came to me and said
I want you to take her.
How can I, I said,
you know I'm not free
and even if I were
doesn't the lady have a vote?
He shook his great head.
She will do what I say;
when I was alive
she never refused me.
How much less will she now
when I am no more,
when my only covering
are the tatters of your dream.

PLEIADES A JOURNAL OF NEW WRITING

DEPARTMENT OF ENGLISH • CENTRAL MISSOURI STATE UNIVERSITY • WARRENSBURG • MISSOURI 64093 • 660-543-8106

5/28/04

Dear Pleiades reviewers—

Enclosed: Copies of at least some of the books you requested. (Many books were requested two, three, even five times, so I've tried to divide things up fairly.)

Please feel free to keep these and, if there are others you want, to request more. I can always get you review books directly from the publishers if they don't appear on the quarterly book lists I send around.

If you want to review one of these for PLEIADES or AMERICAN BOOK REVIEW, remember to call or email me first. I need to add your name and the book title to my file so I can be sure the review isn't accidentally assigned twice.

I hope you're well!

Kevin

II THE NEXT BEND IN THE ROAD

The Next Bend in the Road

If there's a mention of eyelashes, then it's about Osip.
— NADEZHDA MANDELSTAM

The young man with long thick eyelashes is
unapologetically drunk with the world's beauty
despite or possibly because of the hollowness at its core
which he confirms in the slightly dead timbre
of the distant church bells sounding the hour.
Meanwhile the little horses jog onward without
the least appearance of strain, their breath issuing
visibly in twin dissolving plumes of cloud,
and the extraordinarily pretty woman (scarcely
more than a girl) whose head rests on the young man's
shoulder, although she has a husband to whom
she will return, is for the moment all his. Just beyond
the next bend in the road, or if not the next
the bend after that, still hidden by the towering
fir trees, their dark drooping vigorous branches
loaded with snow (I forgot to say that this
is a winter scene, that the youthful lovers are in
a sleigh, that they are both poets, that they will come
to similar ends), the Revolution waits.

Tsvetayeva's Letters

In Boris Pasternak's *Essay in Autobiography* the story is briefly told of how he came to lose almost a hundred letters written to him over two decades by Marina Tsvetayeva. The disaster (my word, not his; by the standards of the time the loss was scarcely an event) occurred during the Great Patriotic War when Pasternak entrusted the letters, along with others from his parents, Maxim Gorky and Romain Rolland, to a close friend on the staff of the Scriabin Museum. The friend deposited most of Pasternak's hoard in the fireproof museum safe; but fearing the worst she kept Tsvetayeva's letters with her at all times, never letting them out of her sight. The denouement might have been predicted. One winter evening, walking utterly exhausted through a dark wood between the station and her home outside the city, she realized that she had left her attaché case containing the letters on the train from Moscow. "That was how Tsvetayeva's letters were borne away and vanished," Pasternak concludes. Stoic toward all concerned he says not a word about the reaction of his friend, the nameless heroine of this exemplary tale, when she grasped what she had done.

The Curvature of the Earth

In Red Square the curvature of the earth is more extreme
than anywhere else, recalled Mandelstam in exile in Voronezh.
By the time the earth reached Voronezh it was nearly vertical
so that the poet and his birdlike wife had to cling to it with their fingernails

to keep from falling into space. Probably they would have been better off
ten thousand miles up, breathing from oxygen cylinders,
armored against the vacuum by primitive space suits,
holding gauntleted hands as they soared above the Kremlin . . .

Not really. And yet the end is pitiful
to imagine: a half-demented ghost with inflamed eyelids and a convulsive
shudder declaiming poems that hadn't been committed to writing
to a ragged circle of men with no names and no faces

in arctic cold by the light of a barrel of burning creosote.
The eyelashes long gone that had been cherished
by Tsvetayeva. What remained, we are free to think, was the hushed
    intent voice
that once had held spellbound sophisticated St. Petersburg audiences

in a doll's universe clock ticks from annihilation. Snow was falling
then too but the houses were if anything overwarm, with cavernous fireplaces,
uniformed servants, elaborate buffets, and on the bookshelves Russian
    and French classics
in the sumptuous morocco-bound editions that crowned immortality.

"The Earthquake in Chile"

Nothing is more remarkable in Kleist than his fierce aversion to the ordinary course of events by which the human race propagates itself—and yet he is unable to imagine simply doing away with biological reproduction. The conflict that results lies at the heart of several of his most powerful stories. In the last page or so of "The Earthquake in Chile," for example, the humane and courageous Don Fernando struggles heroically to defend two unmarried lovers and their small son Felipe against a murderous mob intent on killing all three. But the mêlée has a tragic end: both lovers are felled by colossal blows, and Don Fernando's own young son, Juan, has his brains dashed out as well. Afterward, Don Fernando keeps the truth from his wife out of fear that it would kill her too, but she learns it nonetheless and grieves deeply until one morning, "with the trace of a tear glistening in her eye, she threw her arms around her husband's neck and kissed him." The story closes with one of the most shocking sentences in all literature: "Don Fernando and Doña Elvira then adopted the little stranger as their own son; and when Don Fernando compared Felipe with Juan and the ways in which he had acquired the two of them, it almost seemed to him that he had reason to be glad." I don't know what I would have made of this before adopting my treasure of a daughter. Now I read it as acknowledging the violence and tragedy that are the inevitable prologue to any adoption, and as offering the hope that notwithstanding that history everything may yet turn out, if not for the absolute best (the word *almost* in the final clause is written in blood), at any rate well enough for ordinary happiness.

Reading

The fox said:
"I like reading by colored lights,
it makes the illustrations so much more interesting."
The bear laughed.
"What sort of books are those?" he asked.
"The books *I* read are nothing but words, page after glorious page."
The fox laughed back at him.
"I'd like to see you perform a tonsillectomy," he countered,
"on the basis of nothing but words."
That gave the good doctor something to think about
on his morning rounds.

The New Year

The bear was feeling blue.
"It's embarrassing," he said to himself,
"to be the only bear in the forest who isn't descended from a famous wonder-
    working rabbi,
the only one whose forebears (ha-ha)
were depressingly ordinary."
But the bear was also the sort of creature
who found it difficult to brood on anything for very long.
So he took down his guitar, which he was only just learning to play,
and struck clangorous chords the entire Rosh Hashonah.

Noa-Noa

One day soon after Gauguin left Papeete for the countryside, a young Maori woman found her way to his hut, where she became fascinated by the photographs of European paintings that he had pinned up on a wall. As it happened, the painting that moved her most was Manet's *Olympia*. "What do you think of her?" Gauguin asked (in Tahitian). She answered, "She is very beautiful." Another long, gazing silence at the end of which the young woman asked, "Is she your wife?" "Yes." In *Noa-Noa,* where he reports this conversation, Gauguin adds: "I told that lie! I—the *tané* of the beautiful Olympia!" A few minutes later, though, he began painting his nubile visitor's portrait, acutely conscious, as he expresses it, "that on my skill as a painter would depend the physical and moral possession of my model, that it would be like an implied, urgent, irresistible solicitation." Not to mention the attraction for her of being taken by a middle-aged Frenchman who already possessed such a beautiful wife! Anyone today who, Gauguin's masterpiece in hand, stumbles across this emblematic multicultural *tableau* and imagines he or she can infallibly decode it is living in a dream.

The End of History

The moment's denting inward like a can
the poet wrote in a fever of expectancy
but the line went nowhere, it had nowhere to go.

All around her bullets did their bloody work,
paving stones were heaped up to make barricades,
but the insurrection went nowhere, it had nowhere to go.

She felt she could almost grasp the dialectic
with her naked feet, as it rushed foaming toward annihilation.
But the antithesis went nowhere, it had nowhere to go.

Her lover rose and lit a cigarette; not long afterward he would die
and she would have no choice but to sell their apartment.
Her passion turned inward, having nowhere else to go.

As for the dent and the can, they alone are victorious,
neither the insurrection nor the dialectic meant the least thing to them
at any time, nor the poet and her lover, nor the flower-filled apartment.

The Ring

We can give you, he said,
five good years
we think. It wasn't an offer—
more like a promise

wedded to a curse
in a simple ceremony. A dog named Orion
carried the ring in his mouth

until it was needed.
Then lay down and wept.

A Night at the Opera

for John Harbison

Young women in kerchiefs, terrified they will not be believed, swear they have not been raped. The setting is abstract—a bare dark floodlit stage before the curtain. First one woman sings, then another, then the third, finally all three together. For a time the husbands are taciturn and withdrawn but as the women's unexpectedly vigorous sopranos, urged on by the orchestra, leap up toward the night sky they break out angrily, in clashing discords. The libretto too is minimal, a dozen phrases repeated over and over, on the part of the women passionate insistence that although they were interned and beaten they were not violated, on the part of the husbands unquenchable suspicion, misery, rage. Toward morning the music relaxes and subsides. One by one the young women fall silent. Behind the curtain (we can just catch fragments of conversation, of laughter) their former captors return to their own villages and disappear back into mankind.

The Notebook

I

In the coat pocket
when they dug him
up, a notebook.
Poems.

II

The last lines
written how? Crushed
prone straining not
to breathe—

III

A lark.
Ascending as if on a
wire. Song flooding
the ditch.

The Immortals

Our routine: when Anna's finally exhausted
I "play" taps, then sing the words.
With the lights turned low. Then I kill the lights,
ask one more time if she's okay, and leave the room. On the ceiling
above her bed the nine Immortals begin to glow
in the company of stars.

The Visitor from the Future

for John Womack, Jr.

When in 1960 I along with hundreds of others at Oxford attended Isaiah Berlin's lectures, I knew nothing (nor did they) of the fateful visit he had made to Leningrad in November 1945, of his all-night conversation in Russian with the unbroken Anna Akhmatova, of the once legendary beauty's passionate but doomed feelings for him, of his recent incarnation in her "Poem without a Hero" as the nameless visitor from the future. Toward the end of my first year, frustrated and depressed by the institutionalized lunacy of my surroundings, I sought out Berlin at All Souls to ask his advice. I knocked at his oaken door and the fruity, clipped baritone voice intoned, "Come in." I entered. Then: "Now you must not mind; I know it was prearranged by friends that you should come to see me, but I have quite forgotten who you are and why you are here. Have some sherry." The kindliness, even the interest, tenuous though it could only have been, were unmistakable. I described my plight as he listened closely. But there was nothing to be done. "I could see at once that the situation was hopeless," he said to me years later. The mystery is how he himself survived, no, flourished there for decades—the life of every Mad Hatter's tea party, of countless insipid High Table dinners—after having spent that one fierce, soul-transfixing night with Akhmatova, after having been submerged for fourteen hours in the Real as if in liquid fire.

When You Enter the Room

When you enter the room there enter with you
all the loves of your past, I mean your youth.
They brush up against you importunately, or hover
in the air like small thunderstorms, or dance
attendance on each vivid gesture, as if waiting
to light the cigarillos you no longer smoke.
You seem, and I guess truly are, indifferent to
their existence, which makes them despond, not
because their passion for you was eternal but because
they were men and the picture of you losing yourself
under them is forever fresh in their minds, as
(they keep telling themselves) it must be in yours.

The Essence of Poetry

"Understand, the essence of poetry is not in rhymes, nor in the verse. It is there so that the eyes can be seen, and so that something can be seen in the eyes." Sergey Esenin said this to Roman Jakobson in the Café Pittoresque in Moscow around 1918. The fiery arch-formalist remembered it all his life despite his evident bafflement—what did Esenin mean? For Jakobson, champion of Khlebnikov and Mayakovsky, the essence of poetry consisted in an armory of verbal devices that by deliberately impeding the poetic conjured it into being. And yet in his monograph on Khlebnikov he would soon write: "Form exists for us only so long as it is difficult to perceive, so long as we sense the resistance of the material, so long as we waver as to whether what we read is prose or poetry, so long as our 'cheekbones ache,' as General Ermolov's cheekbones ached, according to Pushkin's report, during the reading of Griboedov's verse." From the cheekbones to the eyes is no impassable distance.

Full Moonlight

Full moonlight beaming down into their putrid shellhole, into Giuseppe Ungaretti's disembowelled companion's gaping mouth, the poet, normally abstemious with words, writes letter after letter overflowing with love. "I have never been so attached to life," he tells no one in particular between sobs.

after Ungaretti's "Veglia"

The Drowned and the Saved

As we read, Primo Levi is falling.
He doesn't cry out or wave his arms.
On the grass outside the barn it's dark
but also light—a full moon floats on a sea

of cottony clouds, and Primo Levi is falling
from the third floor to the ground floor,
inexplicably, and the moon is shrouded in clouds
that now seem like an army of sheep

advancing like a plague, and Primo Levi
is falling, his eyes are wide open, now he is passing
the second floor, and the moon is being carried
away by the sheep who will eat it in silence.

Outskirts of Berlin, May 1998

A station glides by, not yet ours. A clock—not yet time.

In golden, middle-European late afternoon light that, to a non-painter, would seem impossible to capture with the means at hand a boy and his father watch us disappear, their expressions solemn but impenetrable.

I imagine them posed like that—side by side, illuminated
brows sharply furrowed, a heavy, strap-bound suitcase at their feet—sixty years ago. Then and now the air is filled with pollen from the Ukraine.

Aubade

Robin wakes and thinks
I have been here before
but in fact he hasn't

The orchard may be the same
even the branch on which he sings
but the light is undeniably

frailer and more remote
and the wind that displaces his feathers
gusts from a quarter

not mapped on any compass
Poor robin to be so mistaken
a friend jokes not really sympathetically

who would be clear-eyed in the face of coming death

Beauty Regardless

The camel's eyelids
are impossibly globed and drawn
to keep out the sand.

There is beauty in this—
not just of the perfect match
of form to function

but beauty regardless,
alien, excessive, feminine.
The same goes for the camel's foot

which as we watch
flexes but doesn't rise
from its bed in the dunes.

To Lily, a Calico Cat Who Died
Before her Time

Early this morning I dreamed you were still alive.
You had been stabbed up to the hilt by a tiny sword
which my fingers discovered in your breast and carefully withdrew.
I cried angry tears and denounced everyone in the room.
You were covered in blood and looked pitiful. But you were still alive!

The Wound

The following is based on a prose poem by Picasso's friend Max Jacob. In the first decade of the twentieth century, a Japanese youth with a talent for drawing, who had recently lost an adorable younger sister to an obscure illness, left home to seek his artistic fortune in France. After years of struggle he became a successful illustrator for a comic newspaper. Another year or two passed, and a family friend at the embassy in Paris had the seemingly innocent idea of giving pleasure to the young man's father by sending him a collection of cuttings of his gifted son's work. But when the proud paterfamilias spread the cuttings out before him, he burst into tears: in every figure of a pretty girl (and they were legion) he recognized the slender, twiglike form of his absent daughter, whom the young man had cherished and protected all her life and whose death on the eve of his departure was a wound that stubbornly refused to heal.

III A SUMMER NIGHT

The First Morning

The first morning we awoke
together, before I opened my eyes,
I heard the lions in the zoo roar.
Feeding time.

But not for us—we were
sated, our abandoned bodies still slept
in the sunlight flooding the cage
forever.

ll St. Edmund's Terrace
London, NW8

The Flower

One short flight below I hear you and our daughter
passionately pouring yourselves into each other
like two oceans collaborating on a flower.

Last Visit from Ian Hamilton

Without empathy the camera briefly looked the dying poet in the eye and saw everything.

The Hilltop

On a high hilltop one autumn afternoon, three recent arrivals—a fox, an eagle, a rabbit. The fox speaks: "I made my way here by devious paths, traveling mainly at night. I killed only when I had to, but when there was no choice I didn't flinch. The journey took years. I was little more than a pup when I set out and now . . . well, let's just say that I'm middle-aged for a fox. It had better have been worth it." Then the eagle: "I came without forethought. I was flying from the northern glacier to the southern ocean when I suddenly noticed this mound of intense color hundreds of feet below. It looked welcoming, I don't know how else to put it. So I descended. If yet again life disappoints me, I'm gone." Finally the rabbit: "All my life I've been afraid and run from trouble as fast as I can. And of course when I'm running like that my mind is a complete blank, I've no idea where I am or where I'm going, my lungs feel like they're about to explode into bloody shreds, sometimes I defecate in mid-hop from sheer terror. I ran and ran and here I am."

In Seattle

How shall a man know he is in Seattle?
By the seaplane slowly passing overhead.

A few raindrops but not enough
to make him spring open his umbrella.

The sun not burning through the clouds but concentrated,
opalescent, at their heart.

Hills abounding, scraggly with pine.
An empty barge being hustled by twin red-stacked tugs across the Sound.

The certainty, even at this distance,
that the mountains will have more to say.

A young, coffee-bearing couple in shorts
who practically shout "Good Morning!" as they hike by.

The Yellow Dress

By a whim of the goddess they are sat together at *Phèdre*. At first nothing happens. Then gradually from the hem of her long yellow dress flames arise and, gathering strength from the unhastening alexandrines, become an inferno that engulfs them both.

The Thirty Years War

I understand the landsknechts in their passion butchering the defenseless peasant and his family but why hack to death the cow? A blood-red sun is sinking, against a glacial sky delicately fashioned clouds redistribute its rays, and hovering just above the smoke from the burning barn an angel in princely robes and with slowly beating wings looks into the future. On its cheek a single tear, never to fall.

Freud's Sacrifice

Picture this: Freud at not quite fifty walks through a room in his Bergasse apartment wearing a dressing gown and straw slippers on his feet. Suddenly he yields to an impulse and hurls one of the slippers at the wall, causing a beautiful little marble Venus to fall from its bracket and shatter on the floor. As it breaks into pieces, he recites two lines of nonsense verse by Wilhelm Busch:

> Ach! die Venus ist perdü—
> Klickeradoms!—von Medici!

And goes his way. A lesser man, reflecting on similar actions, might have questioned his own sanity. But Freud explains his bizarre behavior in terms of his situation at the time. "One of my family was gravely ill," he writes (a footnote tells us it was his eldest daughter), "and secretly I had already given up hope of her recovery. That morning I had learned that there had been a great improvement, and I know I had said to myself: 'So she's going to live after all!' My attack of destructive fury served therefore to express a feeling of gratitude to fate and allowed me to perform a 'sacrificial act'—rather as if I had made a vow to sacrifice something or other as a thank-offering if she recovered her health! The choice of a Venus de Medici for this sacrifice was clearly only a gallant act of homage towards the convalescent. But even now it is a mystery to me how I made up my mind so quickly, aimed so accurately, and avoided hitting anything else among the objects so close to it."

Who could doubt the reasonableness of this? However, there is one phrase that sticks out just a little: "attack of destructive fury." My account of Freud's assault on the Venus follows his language closely, and there isn't a hint of fury in his capsule narrative of what he did. No, the fury must reside in the mind's bowels: can it be that Freud had for some time been doing exceedingly painful emotional work reconciling himself to the likelihood that his daughter Mathilde would soon die, and that the news of her unexpected improvement triggered in him feelings that were, even to the slightest degree, ambivalent? *Of course* he was delighted she would live. But just the same—! The sacrifice of the Venus would thus have been in expiation of an otherwise undischarged sense of guilt. Right or wrong, this explanation too belongs to Freud, whose outlaw genius alone makes it thinkable.

Wittgenstein on Green

The question is how many primary colors are there, three or four? More precisely, is green a primary? Traditionally the question has been handled by considering different ways of *mixing* colors—the colors that cannot be mixed, but are the basic components of any mixture, are the primaries. So if we are speaking of pigments, blue and yellow make green, therefore green is not a primary. But Wittgenstein has another slant on the problem. "Someone is given a certain yellow-green (or blue-green) and told to mix a less yellowish (or bluish) one—or to pick it out from a number of color samples," he writes, describing a language-game. "A less yellowish green, however, is not a bluer one (and vice versa), and someone may also be given the task of choosing—or mixing—a green that is neither yellowish nor bluish. I say 'or mixing' because a green is not both yellowish and bluish on account of being produced by the mixing of yellow and blue." In other words, if we start at yellow on a color wheel and move in the direction of green toward blue, we immediately introduce a note of green, not blue, into the yellow. Similarly, if we start at blue and move in the direction of green toward yellow, we immediately introduce a note of green, not yellow, into the blue. And halfway between yellow and blue we find pure green, without a hint of either of the others. Thus there is no such thing—we would never be tempted to describe a color—as bluish yellow or yellowish blue. From which Wittgenstein concludes that green, although mixable by blue and yellow, is a fourth primary. As he beautifully says: "For me, green is one special way-station on the colored path from blue to yellow, and red is another."

In a more animistic universe the color green itself would have composed a poem in celebration of philosophy's unveiling of its elemental nature.

Fear and Trembling

Over and over de Silentio insists
that Abraham is beyond him.
Either that or, in his words, Abraham is "done for."
Reading the Danish genius's dialectical lyric

at one sitting is simply too difficult:
the besieged mind requires relief
and wanders distractedly in the villa garden
thirsting for a fig, which it finds and devours,

then lets the inside-out skin float
down to the gravel path where it will rot . . .
At day's close the setting sun irradiates
the almost childishly beautiful façade of San Miniato,

in the cooling air swallows describe
untrackable figures of double reflection,
and seated at a stone table our mosquito-bitten
daughter sings out "Baba, look!" as she mixes a new color.

Villa Spelman, Florence

For F. T. C.

The news of her illness
is so atrocious, so shocking,
it gelds conversation.

                  What were the odds

against this happening? Millions
to one. No longer will she stand
before Caravaggio's concerts

decanting their music.

Look Around

I

Look around and you will see the truth of what I am saying:
everywhere there is only poetry
that has gone wrong.

II

That's one mood, a powerful one.
And it's not crazy. But it leaves out the almost white cherry blossoms
during the fragile spate of time
before they fall.

Washington, D.C., early April 2001

Marine

Between scudding heartbeats an anchor plunges into the waves,
dragging cleanly after it the long chain of violent sobs that sinks the house.

A Journey

A sunny cool day in late spring.
Windy. On a speeding train, rocking.
From Berlin to Hamburg to look at art.
My reason for going anywhere.

The fields green, flat, now and
then a small community of cows. Sky
dark blue, with gray clouds high up and wispy
white clouds lower down, drifting

toward the rear of the train . . .
In a few hours I shall be myself
once more, in the great room hung with
Menzels I shall plant my flag.

"Le Déjeuner sur l'herbe"

for T. J. Clark

A bullfinch poses in mid-flight,
like the Holy Ghost, above the picnickers.

In a pond in the middle distance a woman
wearing a shift seems, I repeat seems, to be douching herself.

The other woman, naked, seated on the grass
and twisting her rubbery neck to look at us, is no beauty. But try to ignore her.

In contrast the men are expendable. There is nothing
going on in their heads, their gestures are vacuous, their wide-open eyes gleam
    meaninglessly.

Only their brilliant accoutrements reward our attention,
especially the clay-gray trousers, miniature cane, rose cravat and black pillbox
    cap of the type on the right.

In the lower left corner an angry calligraphic frog
wonders why these stilted Parisian nobodies have invaded his bright green
    woodland world.

It was a moment in the history of the art of painting
when the weight of the broken water rushing out to sea exactly counter-
    balanced the force of the waves rushing in.

No matter how hard we try we cannot imagine
actually entering that space, partaking of that food, breathing that nonexistent
    air.

When at the age of eighteen I first stood staring and breathless in the Jeu
    de Paume
what most astounded me was that the paint appeared still wet.

"Flesh"

The last summer of his life Maurice Merleau-Ponty broke off work on *The Visible and the Invisible,* which was left unfinished when he died, to write the third of his great essays on painting, "Eye and Mind." At its heart is the intuition, at once luminous and obscure, that primordially there is no difference (no difference *yet*) between seer and seen. Merleau-Ponty's name for that undivided substance or condition is "flesh"—in French, *chair*—and his efforts to clothe his new ontology in language that would not domesticate it give rise to sentences like the following: "Vision is not a certain mode of thought or presence to self; it is the means given me for being absent from myself, for being present from within at the fission of Being, at whose termination, and not before, I close on myself." And: "Every visual something functions also as a dimension because it gives itself as the result of a dehiscence of Being. What this ultimately means is that the essence of the visible is to have a lining of invisibility, which it makes present as a certain absence." Under the circumstances even these impersonal claims become tinged with pathos, as does his almost delirious attempt to describe a swimming pool that on the one hand may be considered a purely theoretical object and on the other can only be imagined shimmering at his feet in the dry Provence glare. "When through the water's thickness I see the tiling at the bottom of a pool," Merleau-Ponty writes, "I do not see it despite the water and the reflections there, I see it precisely through them and by virtue of them. If there were no distortions, no bands of sunlight, if I saw without this flesh the geometry of the tiles, then I would cease to see it as it is and where it is, *i.e.* beyond any specifiable place. I cannot say that the water itself—the aqueous power, the syrupy and shimmering element—is *in* space; it is not somewhere else either, but it is not in the pool. It inhabits it, it materializes itself there, yet it is not contained there, and if I lift my eyes toward the screen of cypresses where the network of reflections is playing, I cannot contest the fact that the water visits it, too, or at least projects there its active and living essence." *Son pittor anch'io,* he might have added in the spirit of Diderot, another not quite canonical philosopher who lived mainly in his eyes as long as there was light.

Yellow Crane Tower

Our last day in Wuhan we are all bused to Yellow Crane Tower—not the original, demolished centuries ago, but a modern simulacrum. Huge crowds, high spirits, everyone Chinese except our little group: eight American couples plus one single mother, all with Chinese babies, most with Japanese Camcorders. Surrounded by friendly attention we climb to the topmost level and gaze out over the Yangtze River, barely visible through the shimmering smog. In its currents Mao swam, trailed by revolutionary multitudes, on its shore the classic poets Li Po and Tu Fu exchanged farewell verses but did not foresee, how could they have, that their harmonious world would shatter and their parting be for all time. Overwhelmed, I clasp my bright-eyed daughter to my chest with both arms, as if history itself were about to tear her away (but of course it is history that placed her there).

The Fountain

I

More rain than fountain water
splashes in the rough marble basin.
Is that bad or good? An index
of exhaustion or superfluity?
I don't know, but I dismount, and drink.

II

Thirty-five years later, and
the question answers itself. Drink
in great gulps while there is time!
A perfectionist thrush practices
the song that he will take to his grave.

III

In the fountain at midnight
the water is at rest,
the Big Dipper floats upside down,
and I can see my future
in the black spaces between the stars.

A Summer Night

Alone confused dyslexic
I sit down where I find myself
in the middle of a field.

Around me the night expands
in concentric circles each
a different color: green, red, purple.

In a nearby ditch frogs
chant their sacred literature
at the bottoms of their voices.

I look up but the stars
are nowhere to be seen. Clouds
churn from skyline to skyline.

It takes a while but my breathing
returns to normal, the colors
contract to a single stone.

As I reenter the barn
my daughter standing at her easel
completes the letter *A*

triumphantly. The conclusive brushstroke
ploughs from left to right
with the force of the sun.

The Smoke-Bush

You once wore your hair that color—
not for long

but it was spectacular
while it lasted. I couldn't tear my eyes

from your coiffure! It seemed
to me (not yet

with you) the color smoke would be
if blood burned for years on end as mine was burning.

Song

The hook twists

against the leaper's strength

against his flight and fall

back into a rising wall of spray

against you

against me

against the very thought

of swimming free

The Winds of Dawn

Never mind who, or what:
let the dawn answer those questions
as it may, let the winds of dawn level their fierce gusts
without favor or compunction
                              until all is swept away.
Within sight of the ships, clothed in solar fire
as I carolled home the bronze spearheads, I was at last the poet
I have always wanted to be.

Notes

Epigraph: Marcel Proust, *The Captive and the Fugitive,* tr. C. K. Scott Moncrieff and Terence Kilmartin, revised by D. J. Enright (New York, 1999), pp. 245–46. The original French reads:

Ce qu'on peut dire, c'est que tout se passe dans notre vie comme si nous y entrions avec le faix d'obligations contractées dans une vie antérieure; il n'y a aucune raison dans nos conditions de vie sur cette terre pour que nous nous croyions obligés à faire le bien, à être délicats, même à être polis, ni pour l'artiste athée à ce qu'il se croie obligé de recommencer vingt fois un morceau dont l'admiration qu'il excitera importera peu à son corps mangé par les vers, comme le pan de mur jaune que peignit avec tant de science et de raffinement un artiste à jamais inconnu, à peine identifié sous le nom de Ver Meer. Toutes ces obligations qui n'ont pas leur sanction dans la vie présente semblent appartenir à un monde différent, fondé sur la bonté, le scrupule, le sacrifice, un monde entièrement différent de celui-ci, et dont nous sortons pour naître à cette terre, avant peut-être d'y retourner, revivre sous l'empire de ces lois inconnues auxquelles nous avons obéi parce que nous en portions l'enseignement en nous, sans savoir qui les y avait tracées, ces lois dont tout travail profond de l'intelligence nous rapproche et qui sont invisibles seulement—et encore!—pour les sots.
(Marcel Proust, *La Prisonnière,* ed. Pierre-Edmond Robert [Paris, 1988], p. 693.)

"The Alhambra": The English meaning of the inscription, which I hope I recall correctly, is: "Give alms, woman, because there is nothing in life like the pain of being blind in Grenada."

"Care": Cf. Allen Grossman: "Mind is a pot ('crazed' is broken), body is a pot (may it not leak, the beautiful body full of assurance), the biological cell is a pot (filled full), song is a pot (full of our meaning, almost unbreakable). Pots are memory-stores (the Greeks stored almost everything in pot form, especially stories of greatest and simplest possibility and the traces of persons, the 'dark myth'). The oldest text in the human world is 'face'—the inscribed ornament of the skull pot. The lamp is a skull pot and, when shattered, 'the light in the dust lies dead.'" ("Note 1. Stanzas on pots.

On pots in general and three imagined instances of pot, illustrating conscious body as in 'WHITE SAILS,' " *How to Do Things with Tears: A Book of Poems* [New York, 2001], p. 93.)

"Kafka's Drawings": See Gustav Janouch, *Conversations with Kafka,* tr. Goronwy Rees (New York, 1971), pp. 34–37. The quoted remarks are cited on p. 36.

"Before a Duel": Some of the details are based on Alexander Pushkin's fatal duel on February 8, 1837, with Baron Georges d'Anthès but others are invented.

"The Rape of Nanking": See Iris Chang's searing *The Rape of Nanking: The Forgotten Holocaust of World War II* (Harmondsworth, Middlesex, 1997).

"The Glare": This poem recalls a week-long visit to Jerusalem shortly before the start of the first *intifada*.

"Gisèle Lestrange": The translator whose breath was taken away is John Felstiner. See his "Introduction" to Paul Celan and Nelly Sachs, *Correspondence,* tr. John Felstiner (Riverdale-on-Hudson, 1995), p. vii. For examples of Gisèle Lestrange's work, see Paul Celan and Gisèle Celan-Lestrange, *Correspondance,* ed. Bertrand Badiou and Eric Celan, 2 vols. (Paris, 2001), II, "Dossier iconographique."

"The Next Bend in the Road": For a time in 1916 Osip Mandelstam and Marina Tsvetayeva were lovers. The epigraph is taken from Viktoria Schweitzer, *Tsvetaeva,* tr. Robert Chandler and H. T. Willetts (London, 1992), p. 127. I think of this poem and the two following as composing a triptych.

"Tsvetayeva's Letters": See Boris Pasternak, *Essay in Autobiography,* tr. Manya Harari (London, 1956), pp. 109–10.

"The Curvature of the Earth": The first line is based on a famous pair of lines in one of Mandelstam's Voronezh poems. The second stanza (of two) reads: "The earth curves more sharply than anywhere else in Red Square, / and its slope is unexpectedly expansive, / rolling down to the rice fields / for as long as the last slave on earth is alive." Osip Mandelstam, *The Voronezh Notebooks. Poems 1935–1937,* tr. Richard and Elizabeth McKane (Newcastle upon Tyne, 1996), p. 35. Behind both "The Next Bend in the Road" and "The Curvature of the Earth" stand Nadezhda Mandelstam's incomparable volumes, *Hope Against Hope: A Memoir,* tr. Max Hayward (New York, 1970) and *Hope Abandoned,* tr. Max Hayward (New York, 1974).

""The Earthquake in Chile'": See Heinrich von Kleist, *The Marquise of 0—and Other Stories,* tr. David Luke and Nigel Reeves (Harmondsworth, Middlesex, 1978), p. 67 (with slight modification).

"Noa-Noa": See Paul Gauguin, *Noa Noa. The Tahitian Journal,* tr. O. F. Theis (orig. 1919; New York, 1985), p. 13. For the original French, which differs in some respects from the translation, see Paul Gauguin, *Noa-Noa. Sejour à Tahiti* (orig. 1897; Brussels, 1989), pp. 41–42. According to the back cover of the Brussels edition, *Noa-Noa* means *odorant*—"sweet-smelling" or "fragrant"—in Tahitian.

"The Notebook": "Miklós Radnóti was one of Hungary's leading twentieth-century poets. Of Jewish descent, he was conscripted into slave-labour squads during the Second World War. In mid-1944 he found himself in a camp near Bor, in the hills of Eastern Serbia, where he began writing down poems in a little school notebook. As the Nazis evacuated the Balkans, the prisoners were force-marched back through Hungary towards Germany. Few survived. In November 1944, Radnóti and twenty-one other crippled and emaciated captives were shot by Hungarian fascist troops and buried in a mass grave near Abda. When the bodies were exhumed after the war, Radnóti was identified from the notebook of poems in his raincoat pocket." Francis Jones, "Translator's Preface and Notes," Miklós Radnóti, *Camp Notebook,* tr. Francis Jones (Todmorden, Lancs., England, 2000), p. 9.

"The Visitor from the Future": On Berlin's meeting with Akhmatova see Michael Ignatieff, *Isaiah Berlin: A Life* (London, 2000), pp. 148–69. According to Ignatieff, "[Berlin] never doubted that his visit to Akhmatova was the most important event in his life" (p. 168).

"The Essence of Poetry": The two citations are taken from Roman Jakobson, *My Futurist Years,* ed. Bengt Jangfeldt and Stephen Rudy, tr. Stephen Rudy (New York, 1997), pp. 49 and 174–75 (with minor changes).

"Full Moonlight": Not a translation but a response to and a reimagining of one of the great short lyric poems of the twentieth century, written in the trenches during the First World War. I first became possessed by "Veglia" when I was twenty-one and in Rome; thirty-eight years later, walking in Berlin, the first words of the present poem came to me. The original reads:

Veglia
Cima Quattro il 23 dicembre 1915

Un intera nottata
buttato vicino
a un compagno
massacrato
con la sua boca
digrignata
volta al plenilunio
con la congestione
delle sue mani
penetrata
nel mio silenzio
ho scritto
lettere piene d'amore

Non sono mai stato
tanto
attaccato alla vita

Giuseppe Ungaretti, *Vita d'un uomo. 106 poesie 1914–1960* (Milan, 1992), p. 20.

"The Drowned and the Saved": The English title of Primo Levi's last (and darkest) book. On April 11, 1987 Levi died after falling to the bottom of the staircase of the building in Turin in which he was born; it is widely thought he committed suicide. See, in addition to *The Drowned and the Saved,* tr. Raymond Rosenthal (New York, 1988), Myriam Anissimov, *Primo Levi: Tragedy of an Optimist,* tr. Steve Cox (Woodstock, NY, 1998).

"The Wound": Based on (more precisely, taking its point of departure from) Max Jacob, "Famille Japonaise," *Le Cornet à dés* (orig. 1916; Paris, 1967), p. 210.

"Freud's Sacrifice": See Sigmund Freud, *The Psychopathology of Everyday Life,* The Standard Edition of the Complete Psychological Works of Sigmund Freud, tr. James Strachey, 24 vols, 6 (London, 1960), p. 169.

"Wittgenstein on Green": The question whether or not green is a primary color engages Ludwig Wittgenstein at several points in *Remarks on Color,* ed. G. E. M. Anscombe, tr. Linda L. McAlister and Margarete Schättle (Berkeley and Los Angeles, 1978). See especially part I, paragraphs 6 and 7, and part III, paragraphs 26, 27, 39, 40, and 111.

"Fear and Trembling": An early work by Søren Kierkegaard, who published it under the

pseudonym Johannes de Silentio and designated it a "dialectical lyric" on the title page. The translation I have used is by Alastair Hannay (Harmondsworth, Middlesex, 1985). The notion of "double reflection" also comes from Kierkegaard's writings, where of course it has a different meaning than in the poem. "Baba," my daughter tells me, is Chinese for "Dad."

"For F. T. C.": The initials belong to Franca Trinchieri Camiz, a distinguished art historian (and fellow graduate student at Harvard in the early 1960s) who died in Rome in 1998 of mad cow's disease. Her best known work deals with the role of music in Caravaggio's paintings.

"A Journey": The "great room hung with / Menzels" is in the Hamburg Kunsthalle. Adolph Menzel (1815–1905) is one of the two greatest German painters and draftsmen of the nineteenth century (the other being Caspar David Friedrich). On Menzel see my recent book, *Menzel's Realism: Art and Embodiment in Nineteenth-Century Berlin* (London and New Haven, 2002).

"Last Visit from Ian Hamilton": The British poet Ian Hamilton, author of *The Visit* (London, 1970), *Fifty Poems* (London, 1988), and *Sixty Poems* (London, 1998), died of cancer on December 27, 2001 at the age of 63.

"'Le Déjeuner sur l'herbe'": Before its present installation in the unfortunate Musée d'Orsay, the *Déjeuner* hung radiantly for many years in the Jeu de Paume, along with numerous other works by Edouard Manet and his successors, the Impressionists. Toward the end of my book *Manet's Modernism, or, The Face of Painting in the 1860s* (Chicago and London, 1996), I write: "If it were practicable—it isn't—this book would conclude by returning once more to the *Déjeuner*, the summa and epitome of the young Manet's dream of painting" (p. 401). I think of the present poem as belatedly enacting that return.

"'Flesh'": See Maurice Merleau-Ponty, *The Visible and the Invisible,* ed. Claude Lefort, tr. Alphonso Lingis (Evanston, IL, 1968); and *idem,* "Eye and Mind," tr. Carleton Dallery, in *The Primacy of Perception and Other Essays,* ed. James M. Edie (Evanston, IL, 1964), pp. 182, 186, 187 (with slight modifications). For the original French see Merleau-Ponty, *Oeil et esprit* (orig. 1964; Paris, 1985), pp. 70–71, 81, 85. *Son pittor anch'io,* "I too am a painter," was remarked by Denis Diderot in connection with his intensely pictorial novel (if that is what is), *La Religieuse.*

"The Fountain": The first stanza appeared as an independent poem, "More Rain than Fountain Water," in Michael Fried, *Powers* (London, 1973), p. 50.